SEASONS BY SIMI

SIMI RAGHAVAN

Copyright © 2017 Simi Raghavan

All rights reserved. No part of this book may be reproduced or transmitted in any form, by any means, electronic or mechanical, including photocopying, scanning and recording, or by any information storage and retrieval system, without permission in writing from the creator.

ISBN-13: 978-1975616489
ISBN-10: 1975616480

Other books by Artist Simi Raghavan:

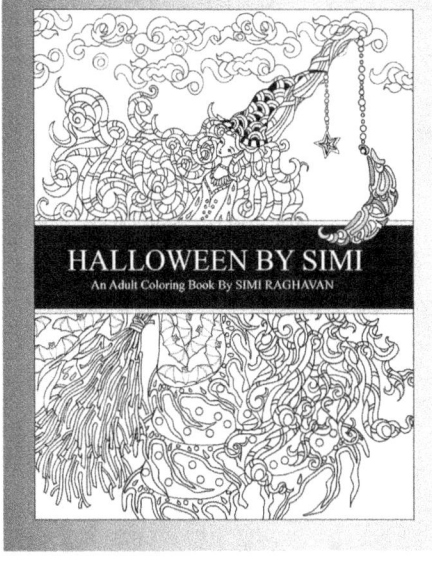

Halloween by Simi
Available on:
www.amazon.com/dp/1537508563/
PDF: https://gum.co/halloweenbysimi

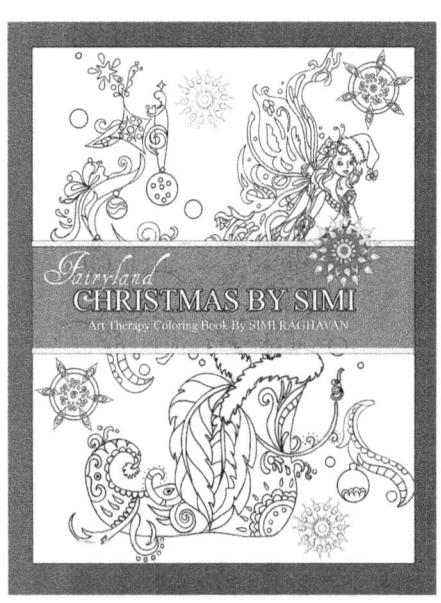

Fairyland Christmas by Simi
Available on:
www.amazon.com/dp/1534995420/
PDF: https://gum.co/fairylandchristmasbysimi

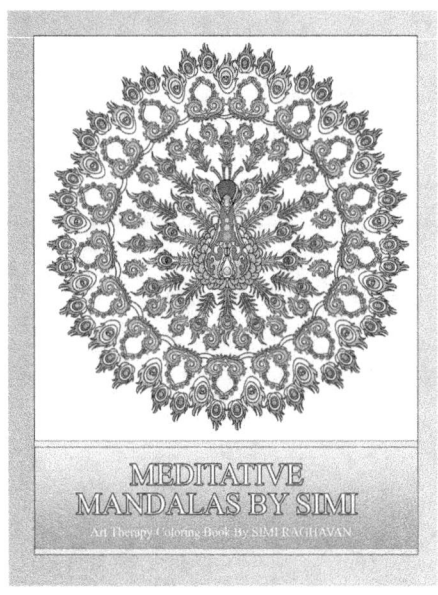

Meditative Mandalas by Simi:
www.amazon.com/dp/1542355079
PDF:https://gum.co/meditativemandalasbysimi
www.createspace.com/6837395

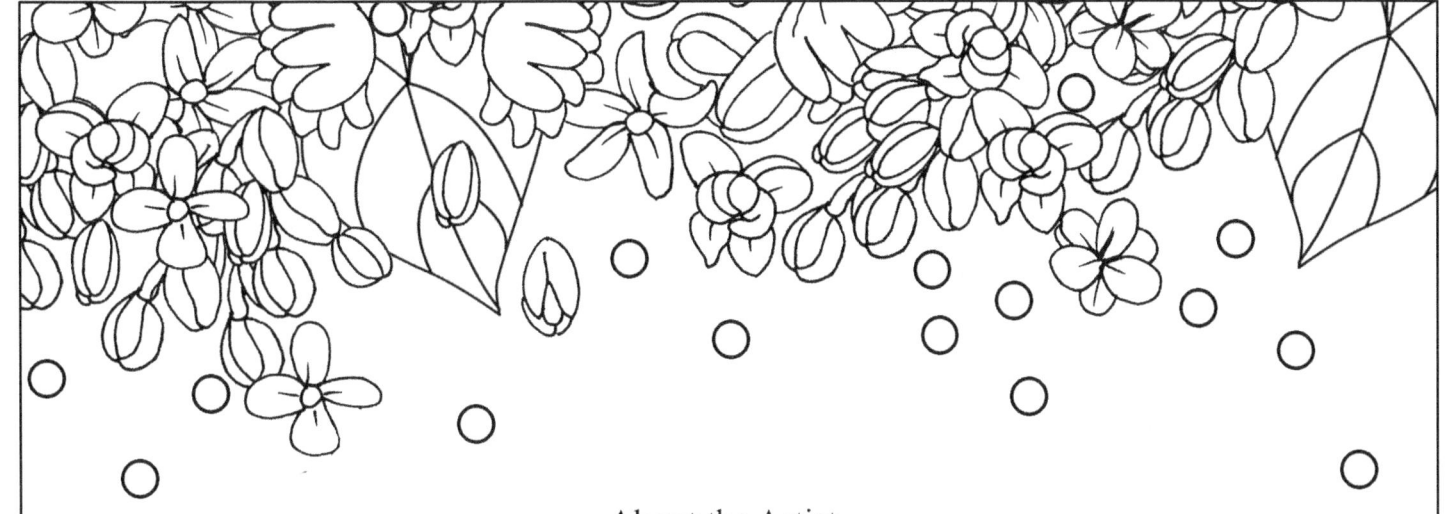

About the Artist.

Simi lives in the exotic land of Kerala, in India. Her artwork flourishes amidst the gorgeous backwaters, the never ending greenery, aroma of chai & spices, mantras & chants from the temples. Everything around her inspires her to create new pieces of amazing art. Have fun coloring, leave a review on amazon & don't forget to post your colored pages on her Facebook group.
Happy coloring :)

www.simiraghavan.com
www.amazon.com/author/simiraghavan
www.facebook.com/simiraghavanart
www.facebook.com/groups/simiraghavan
info@simiraghavan.com

"Seasons by Simi is something I have been meaning to do for a long while now. The changing of the seasons is always a beautiful thing. The season fairies fly in with their fairy dust and do their magic! I hope you enjoy coloring in and don't forget to share your colored pieces with me."
 -Simi.

PDF copy is available here: https://gum.co/seasonsbysimi

Feel free to test out your colors here.

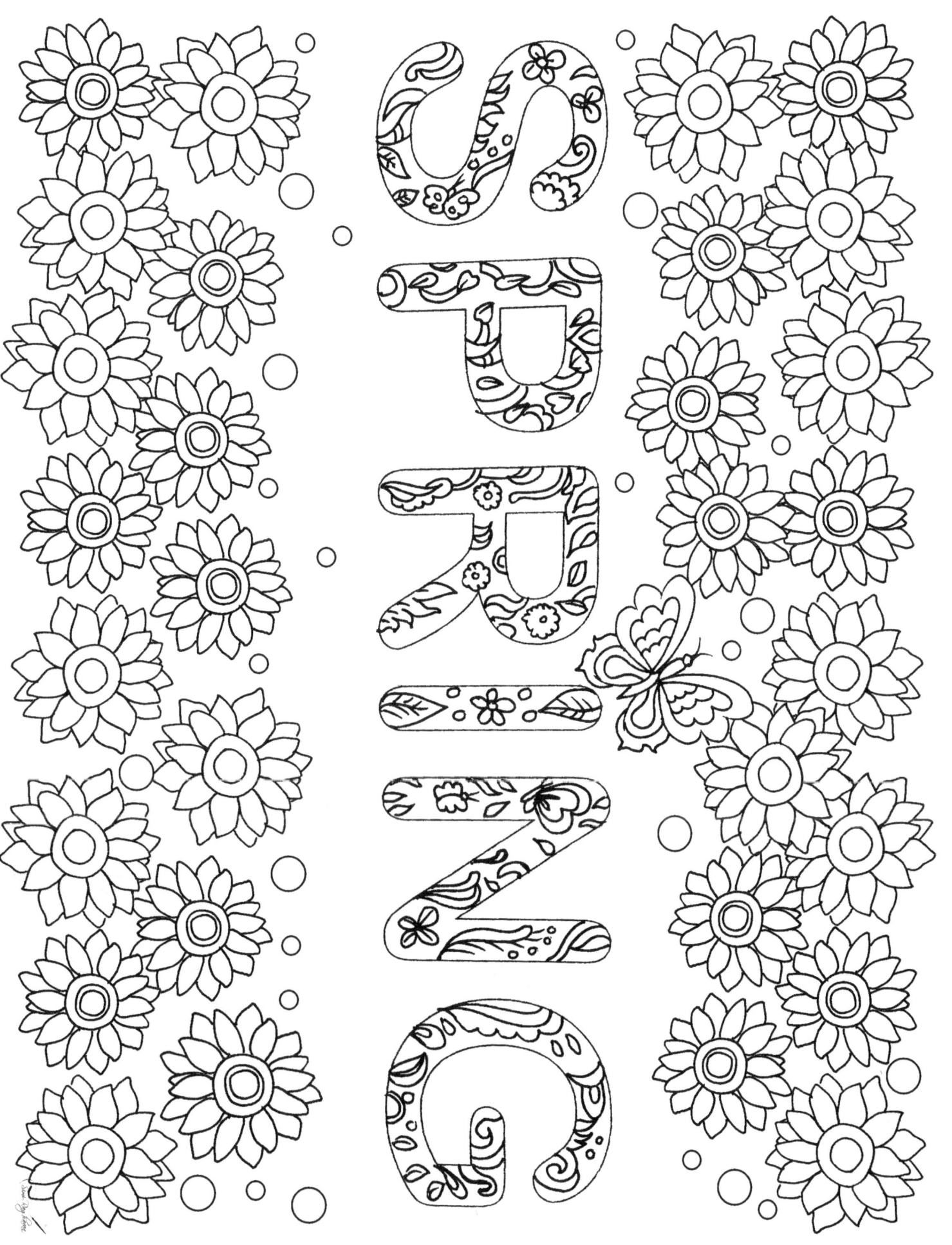

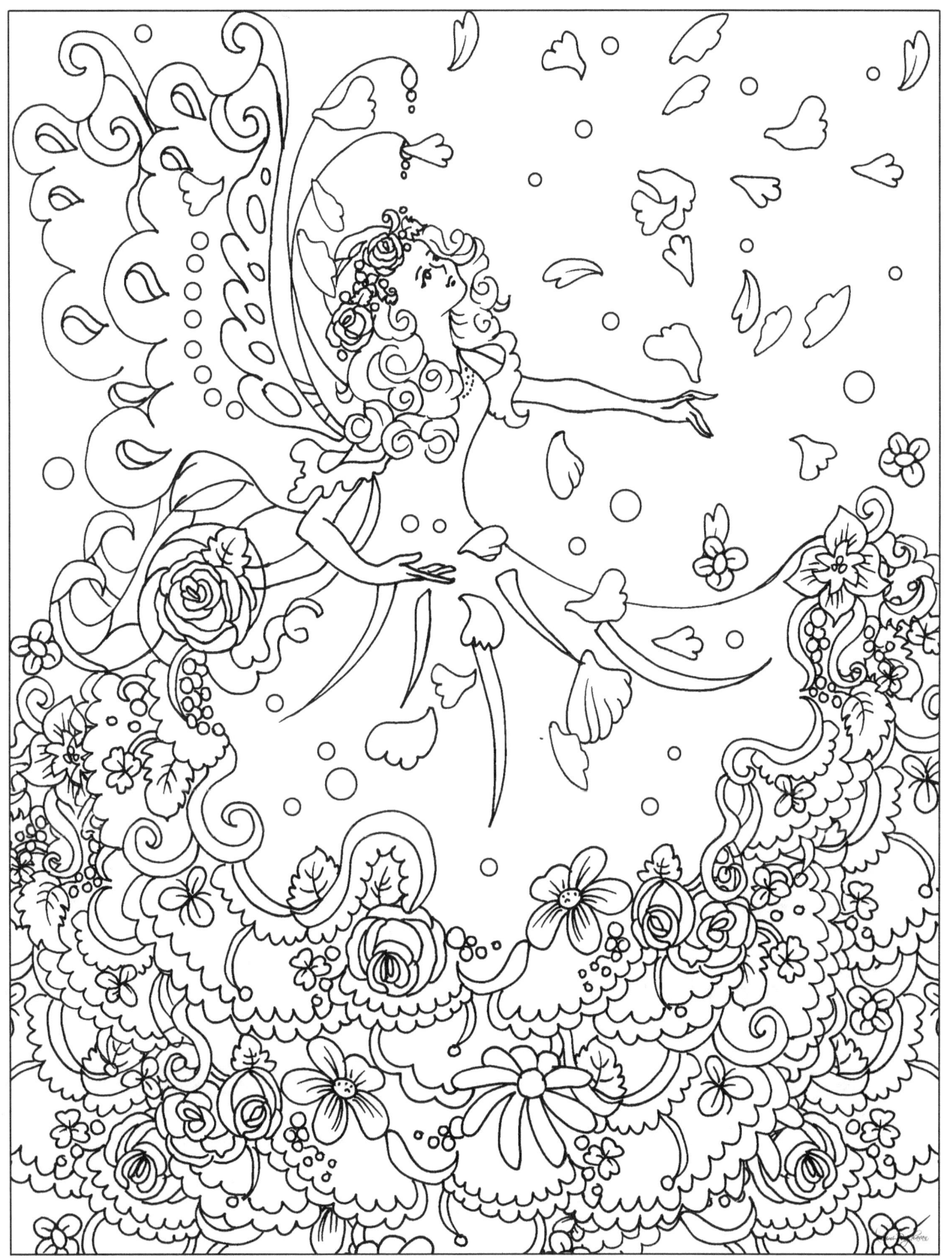

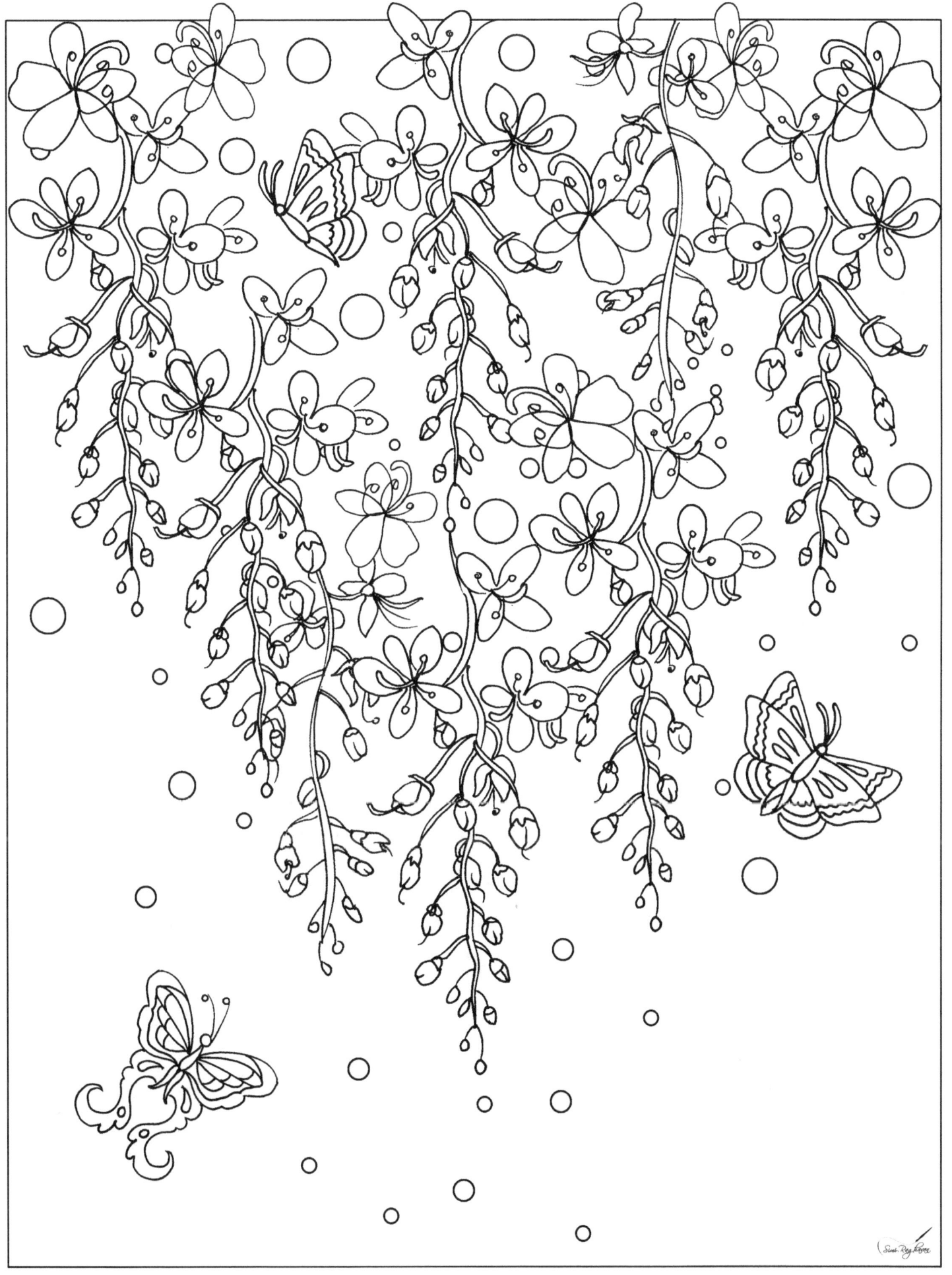

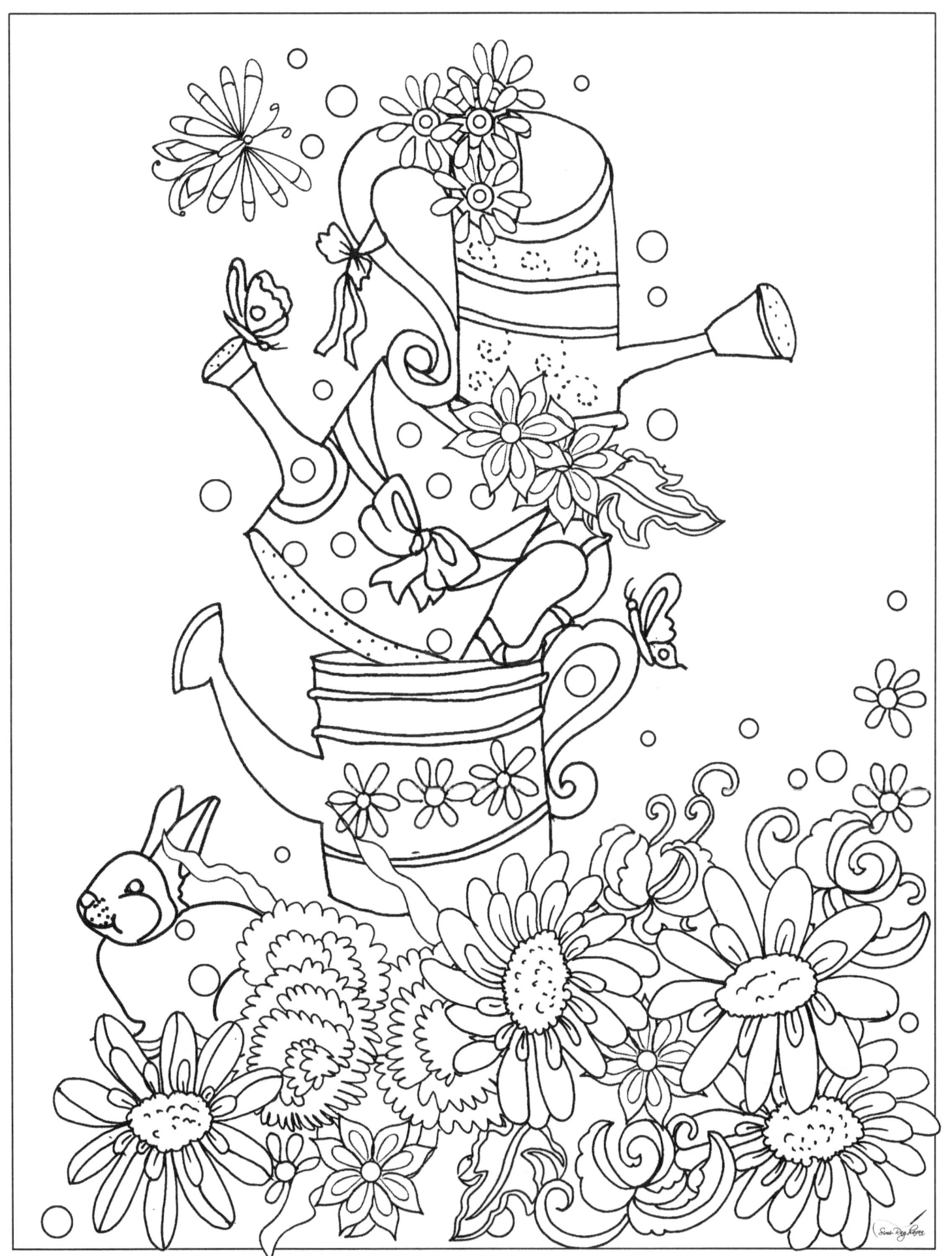

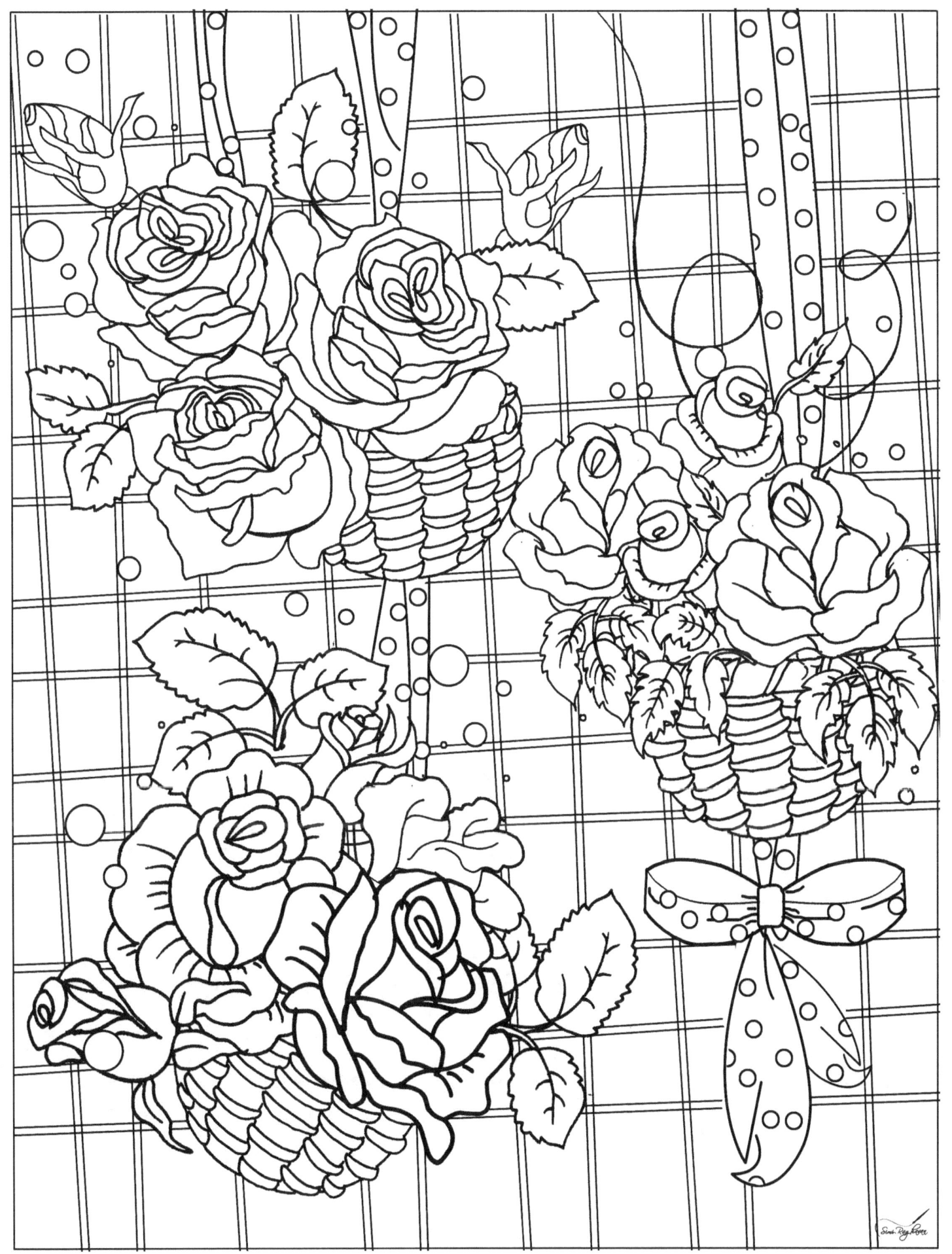

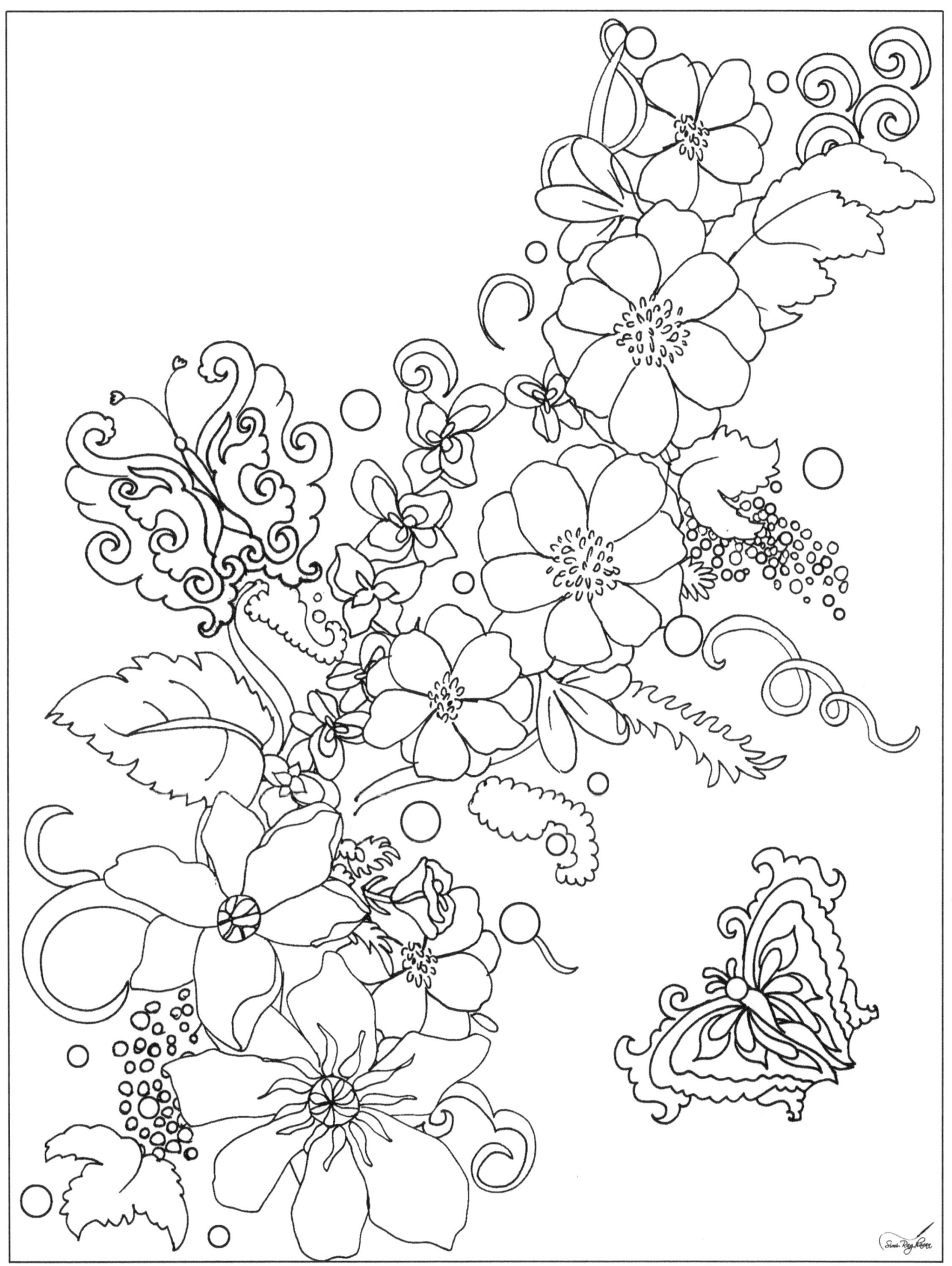

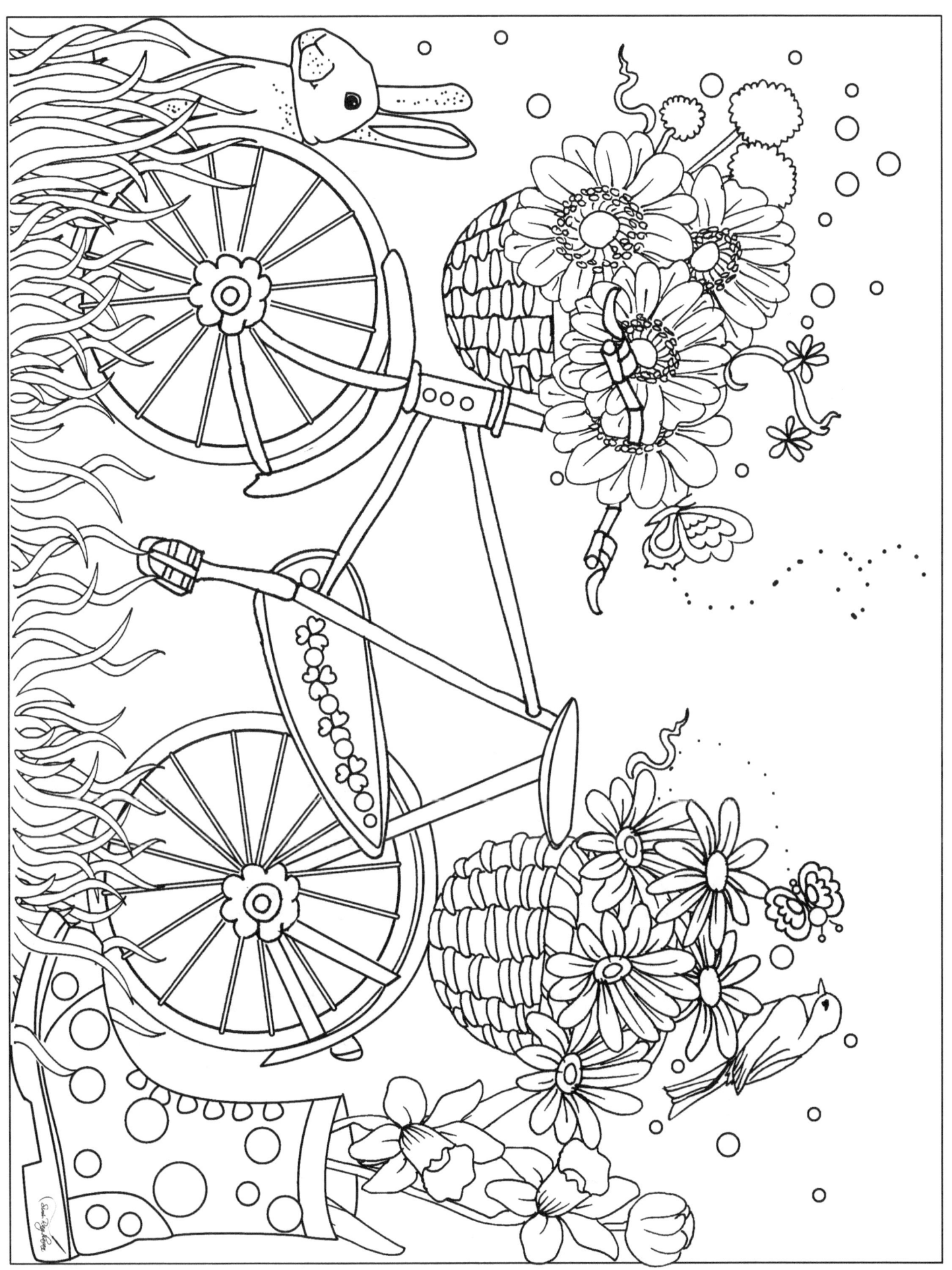

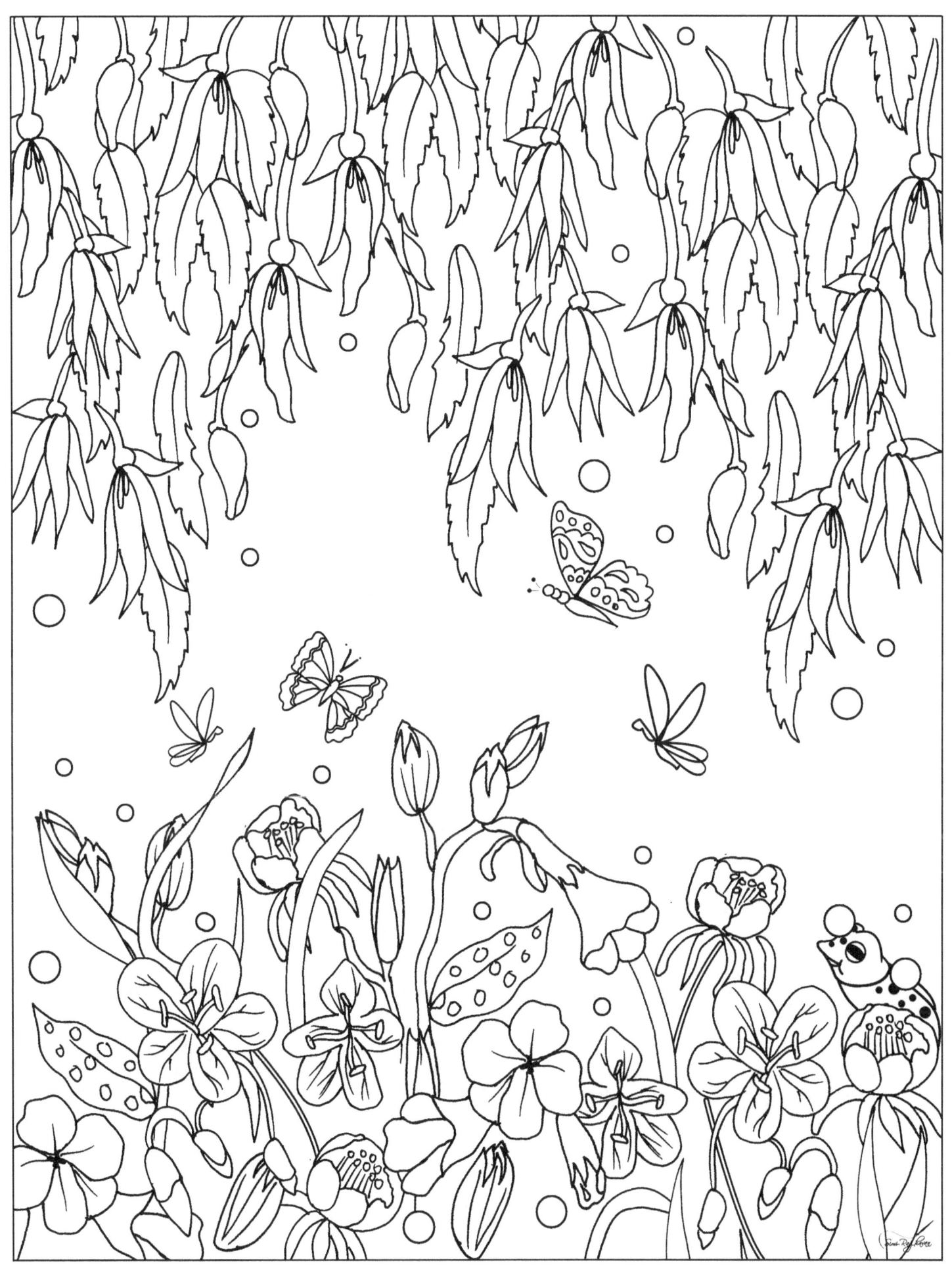

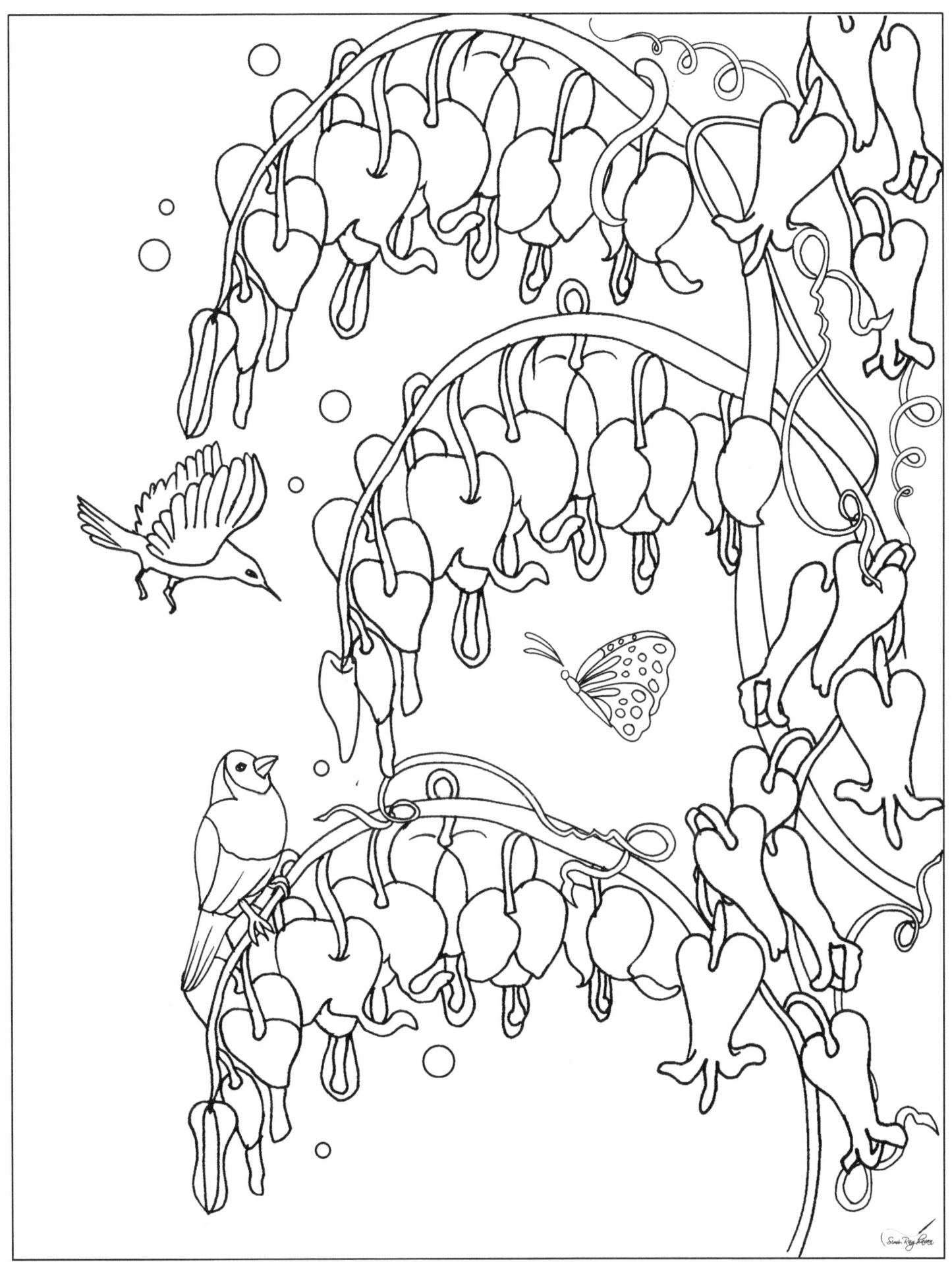

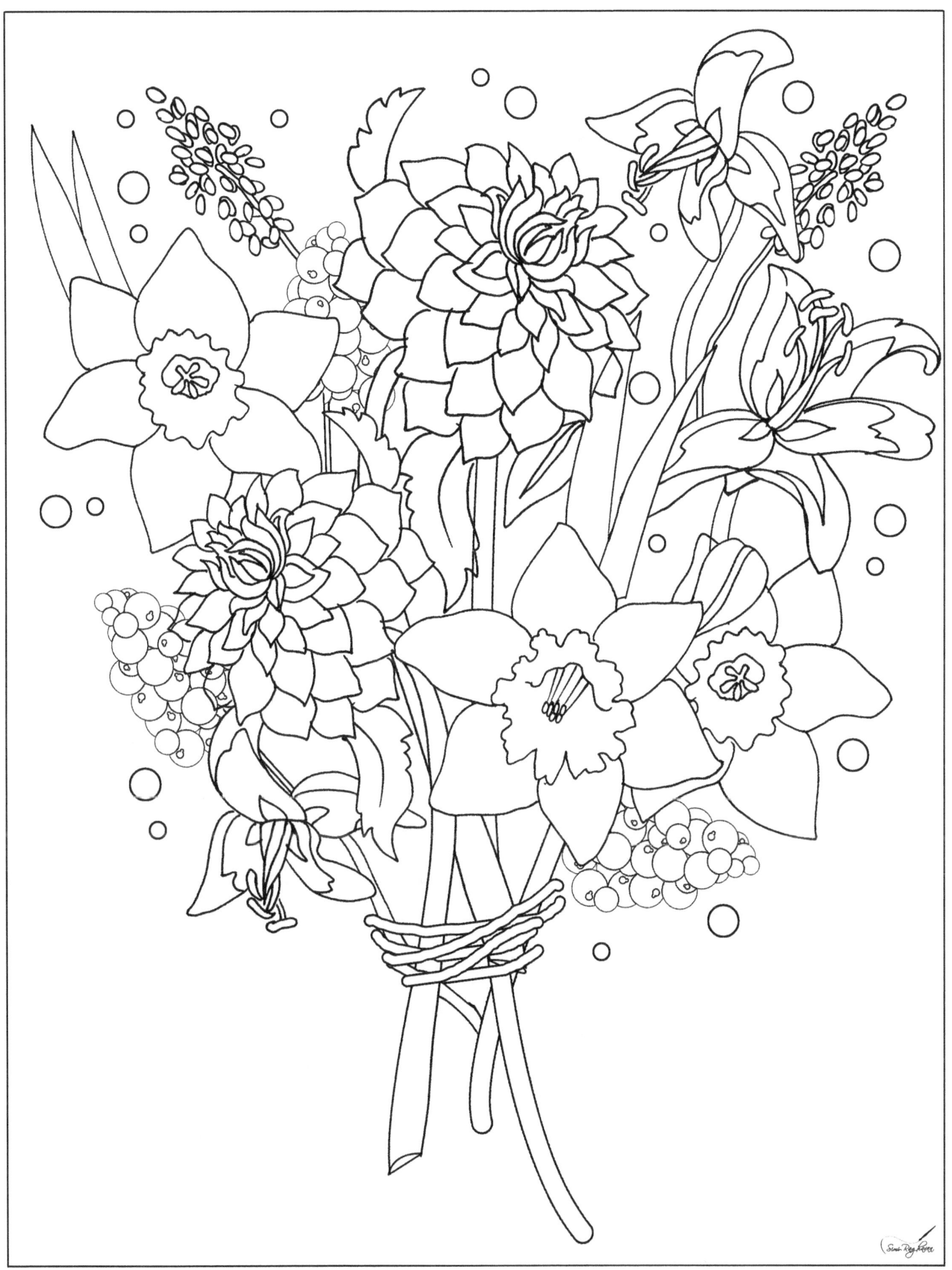

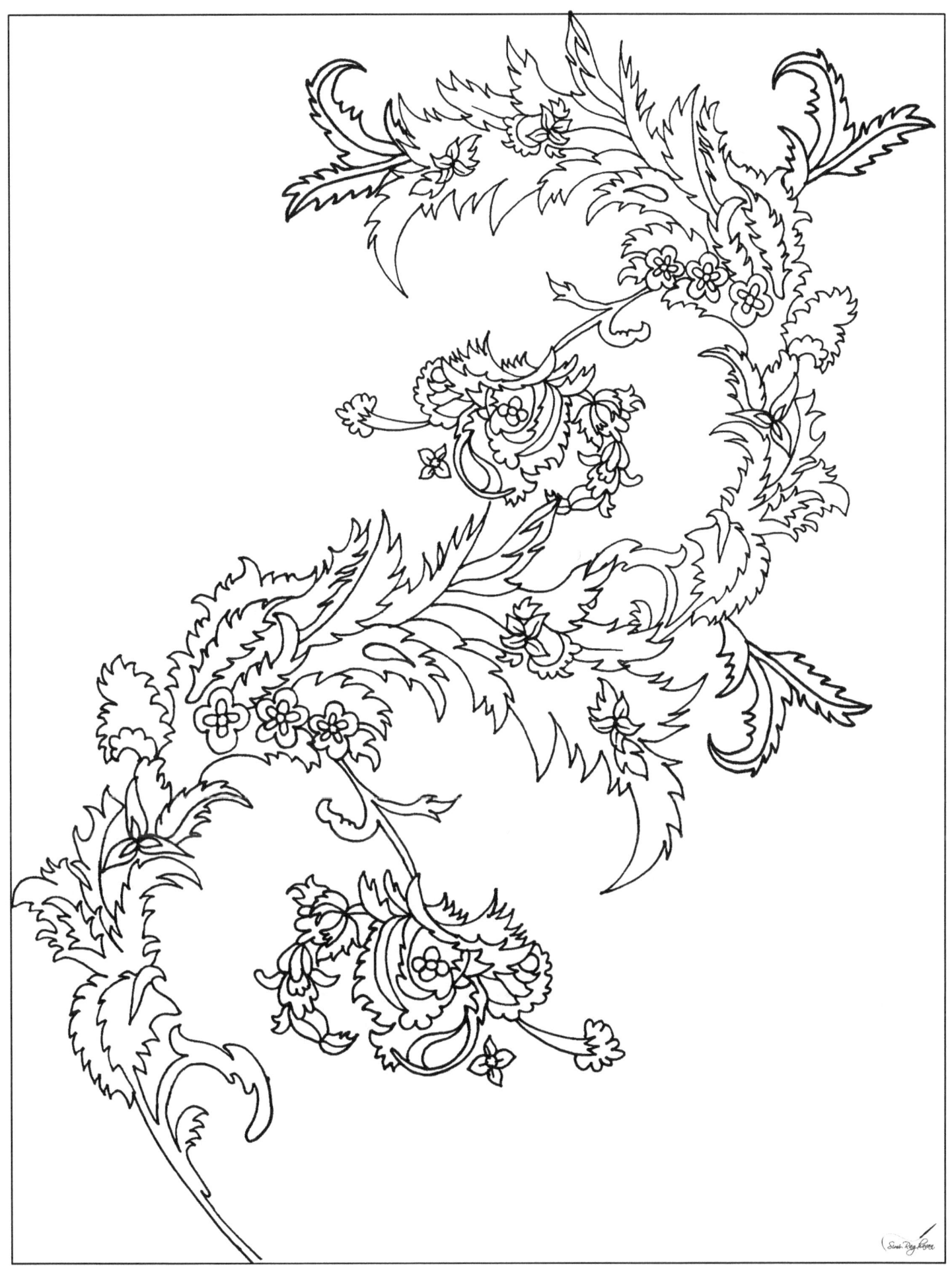

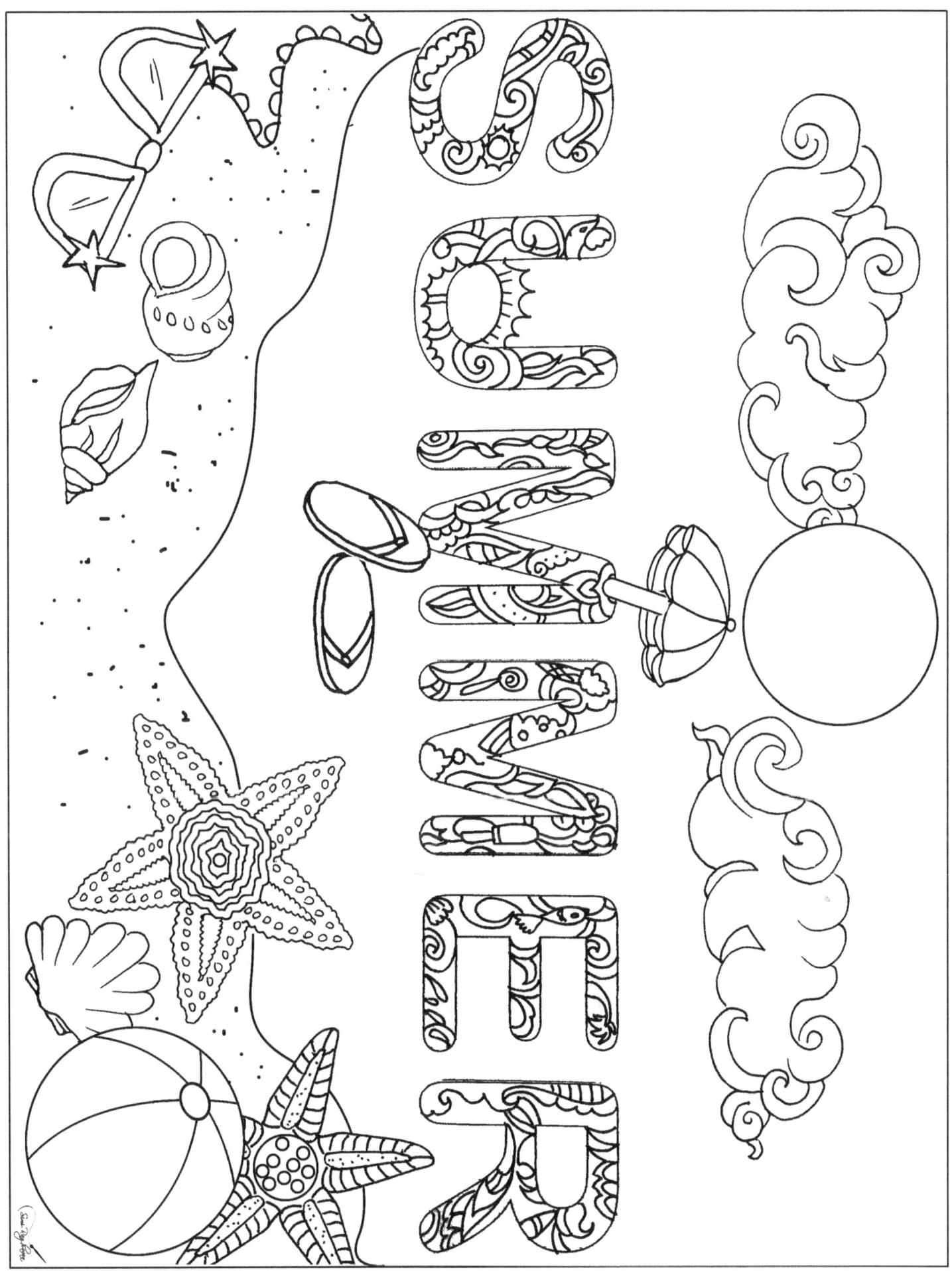

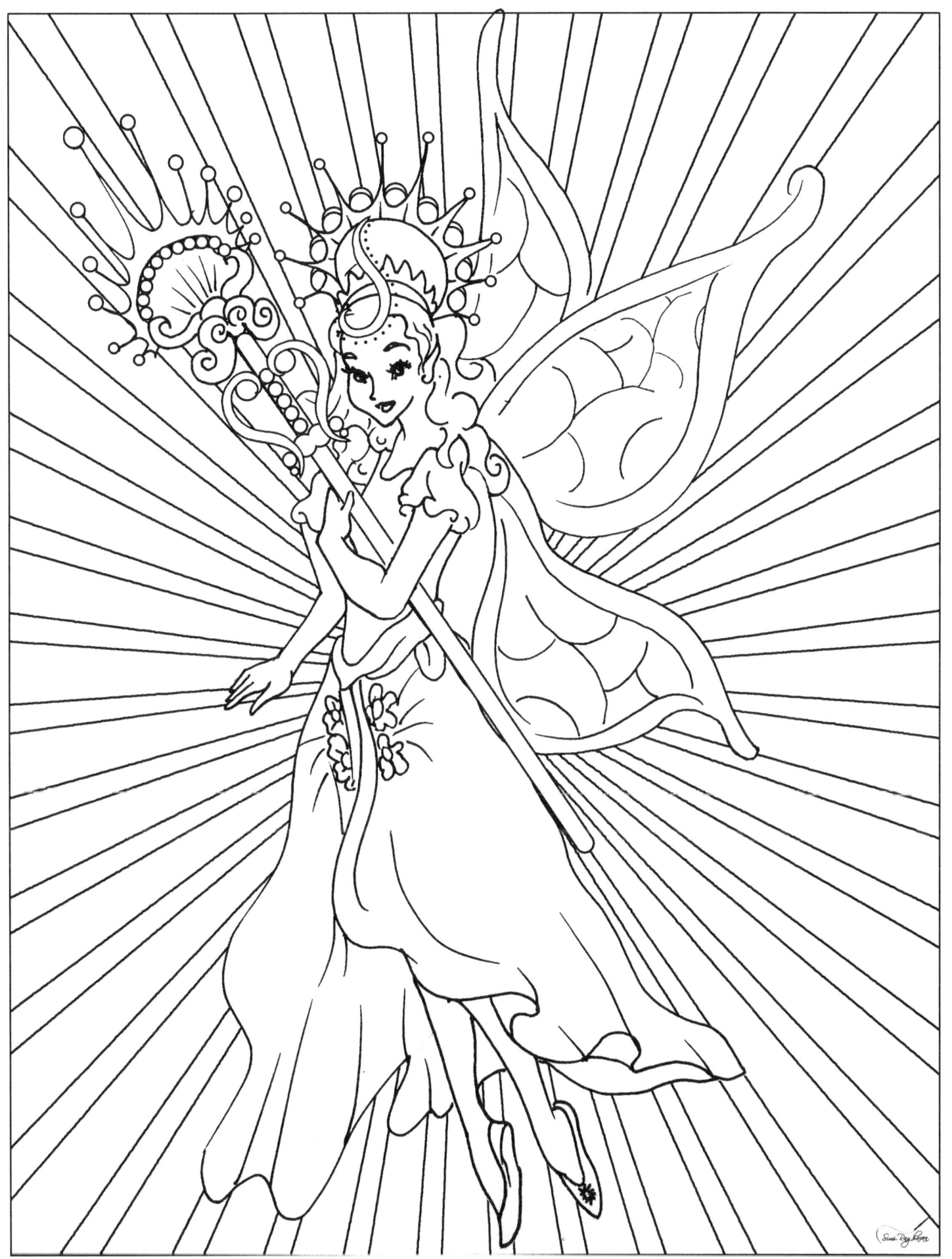

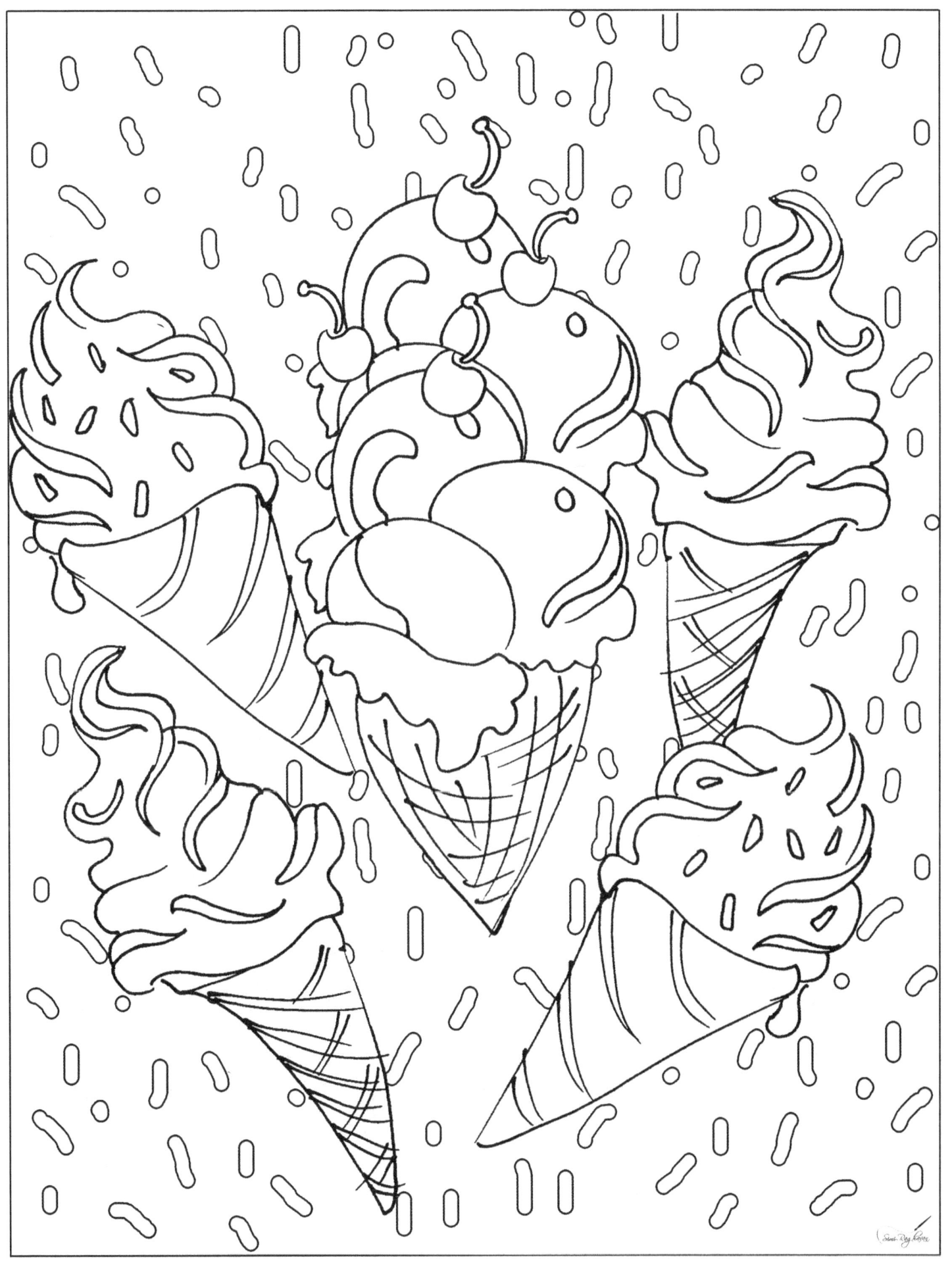

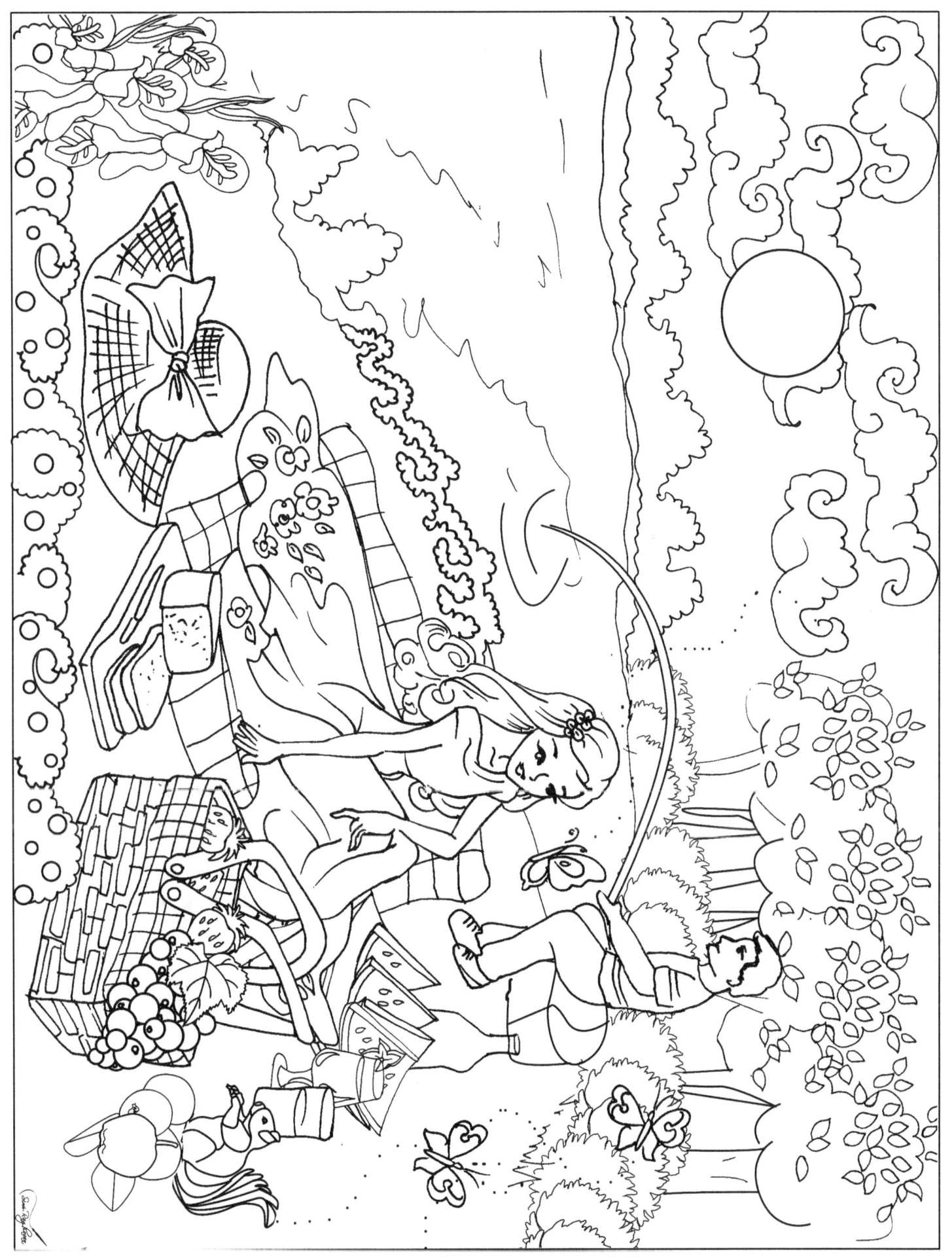

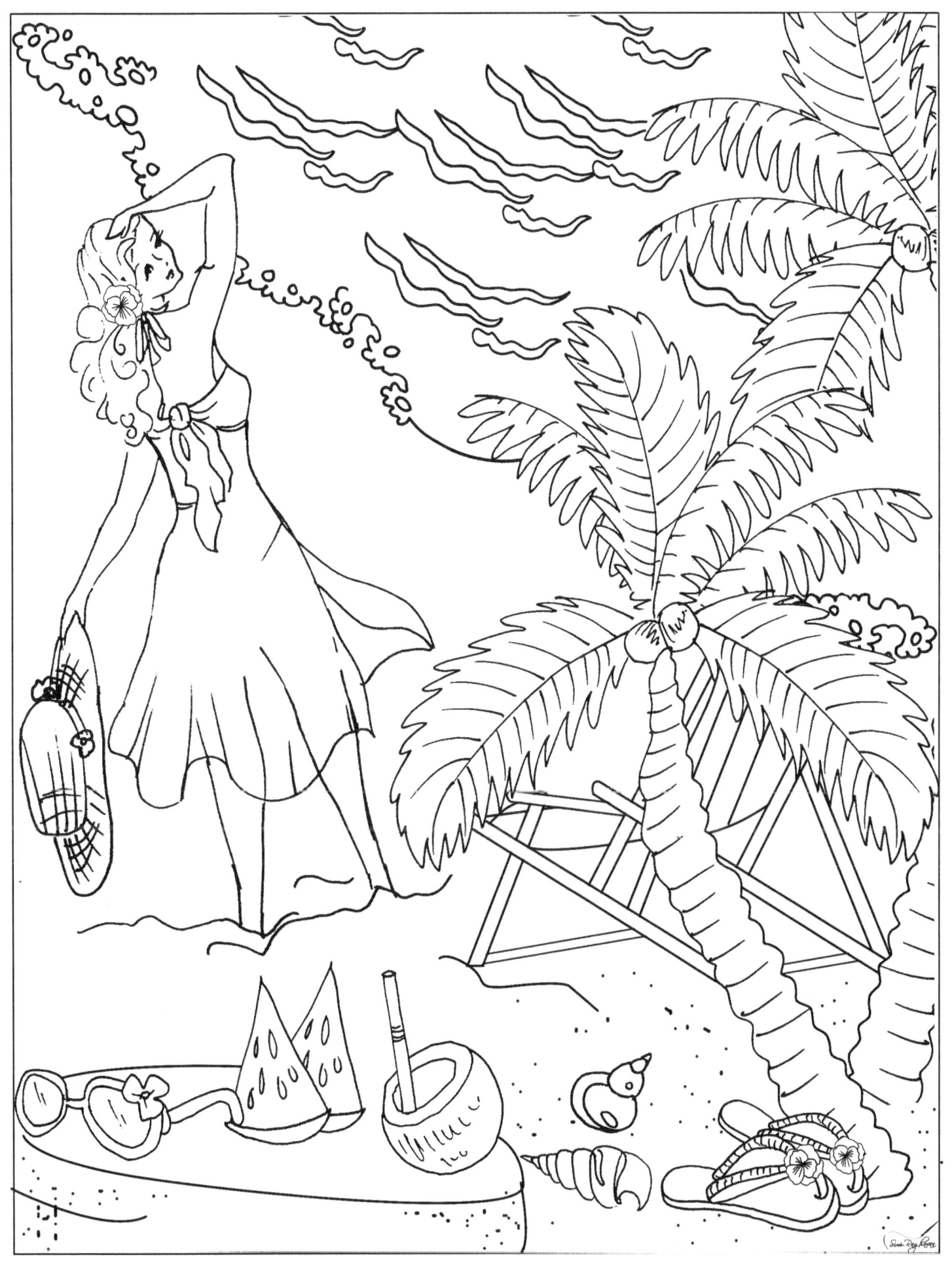

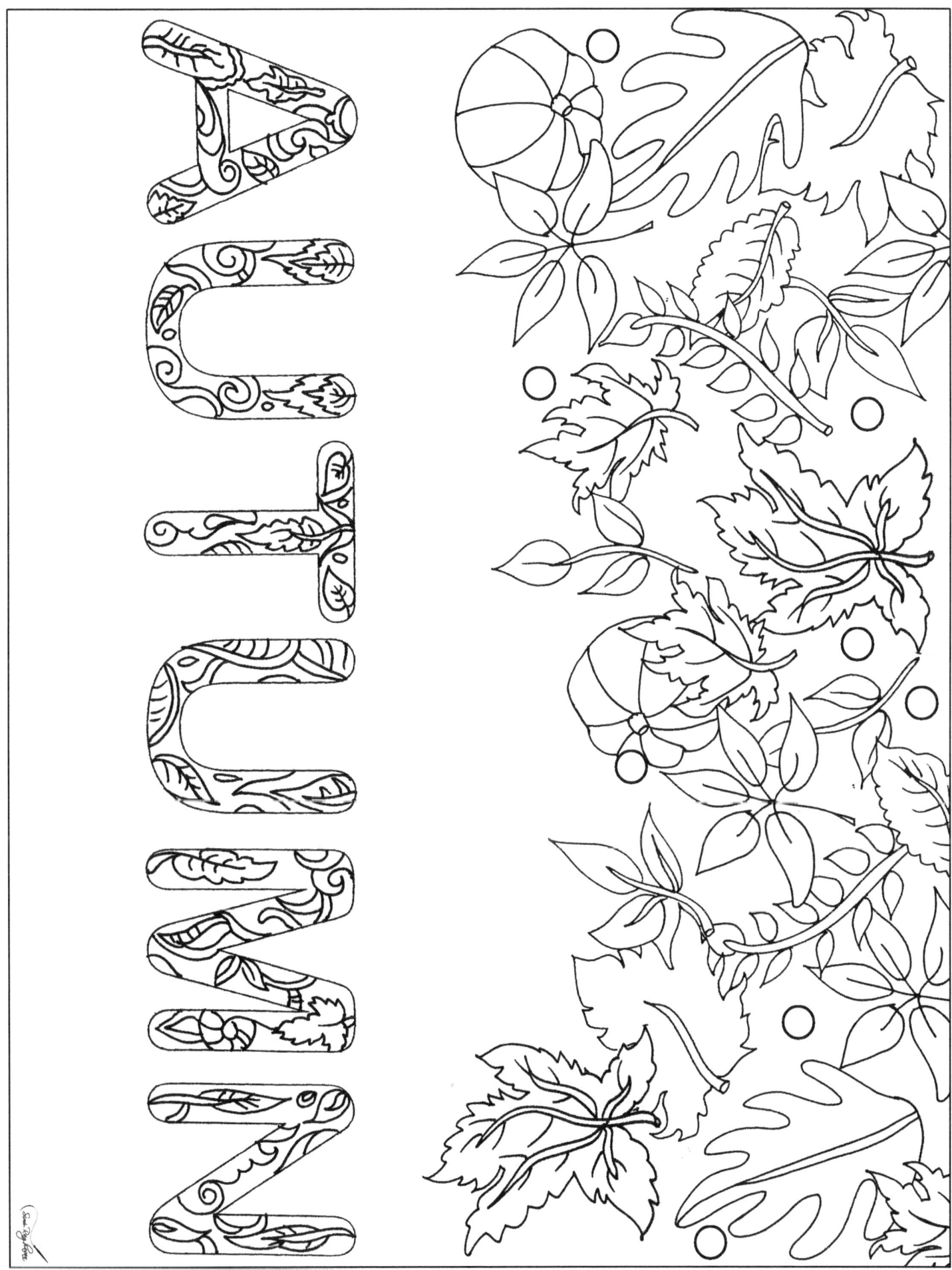

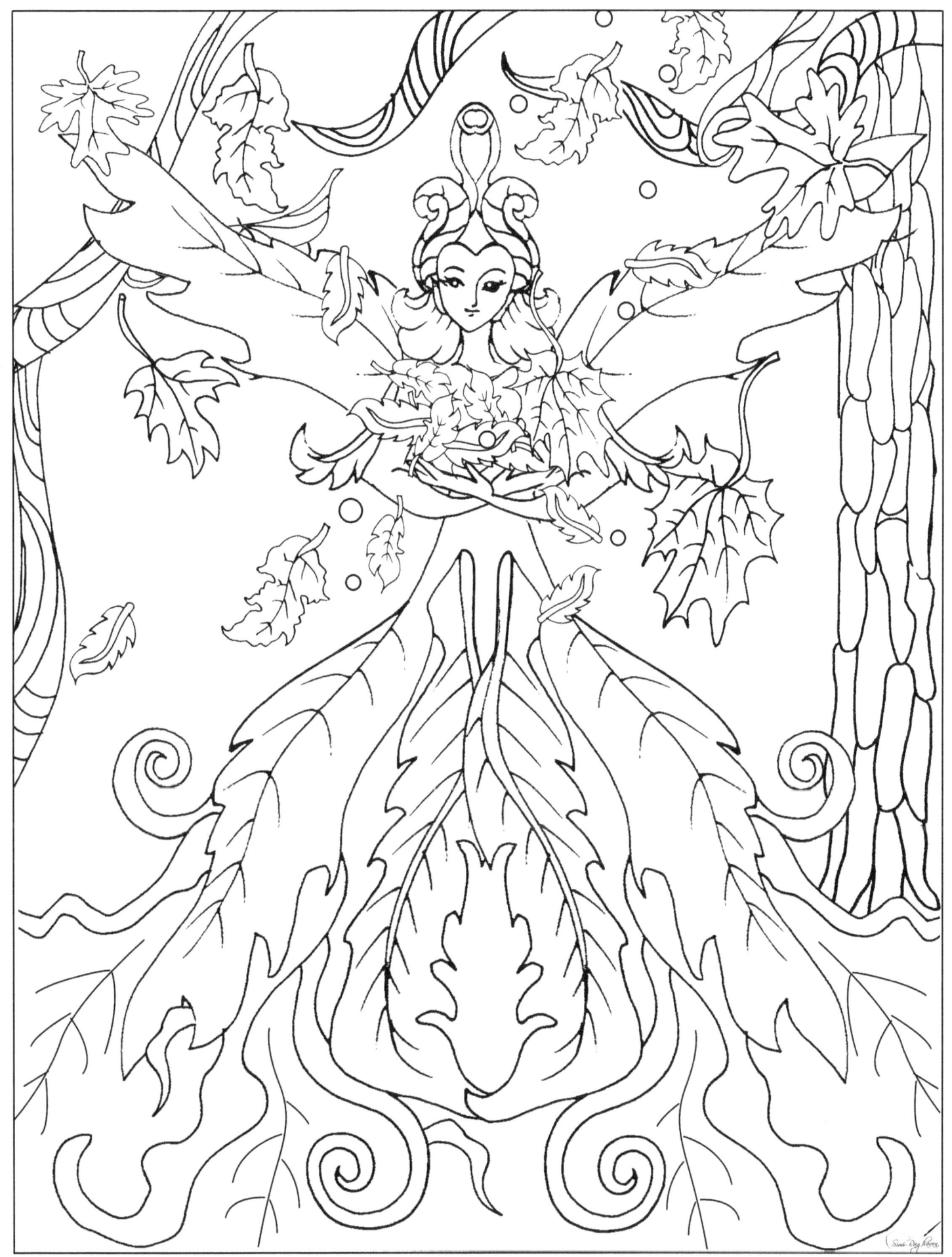

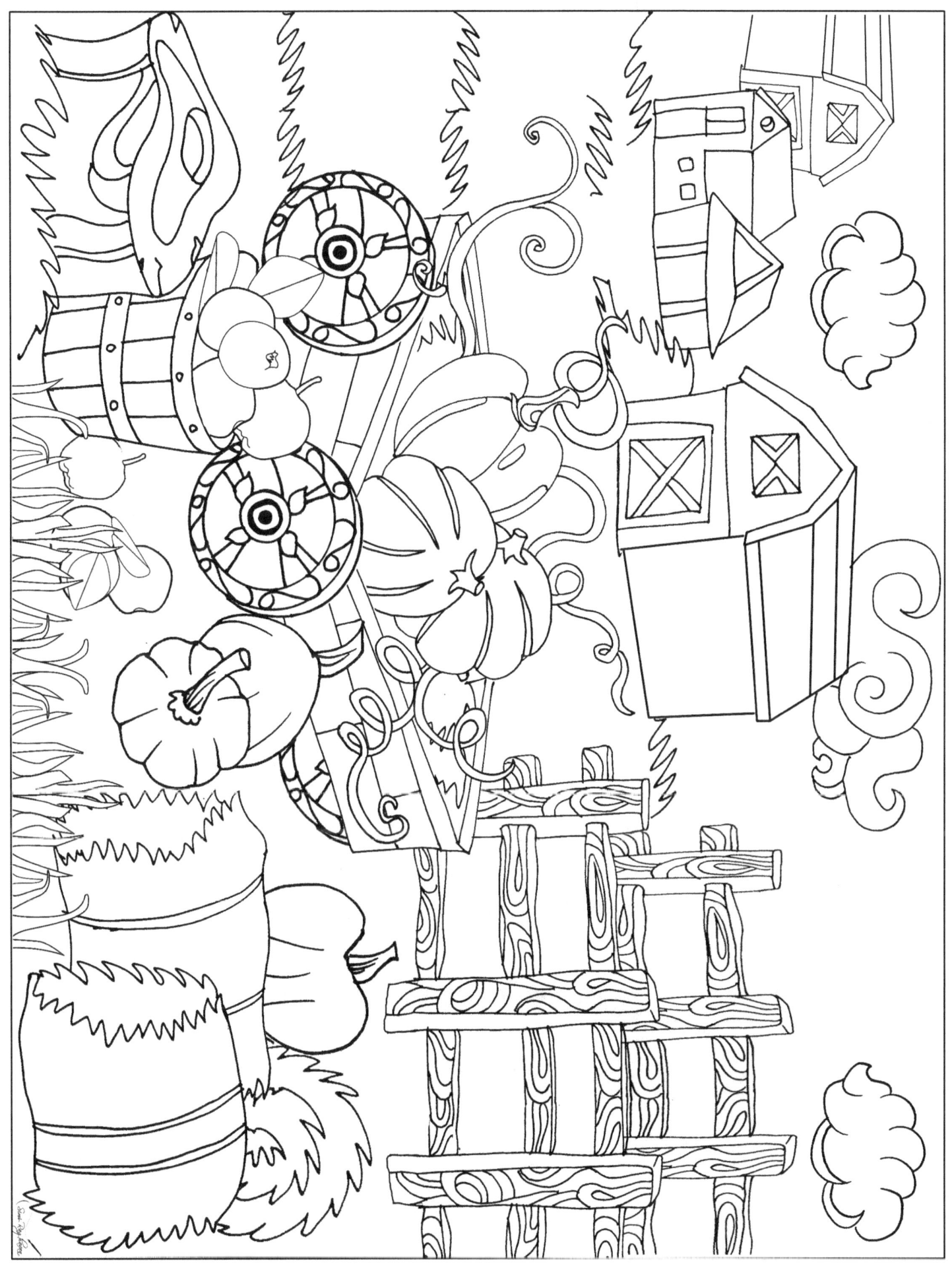

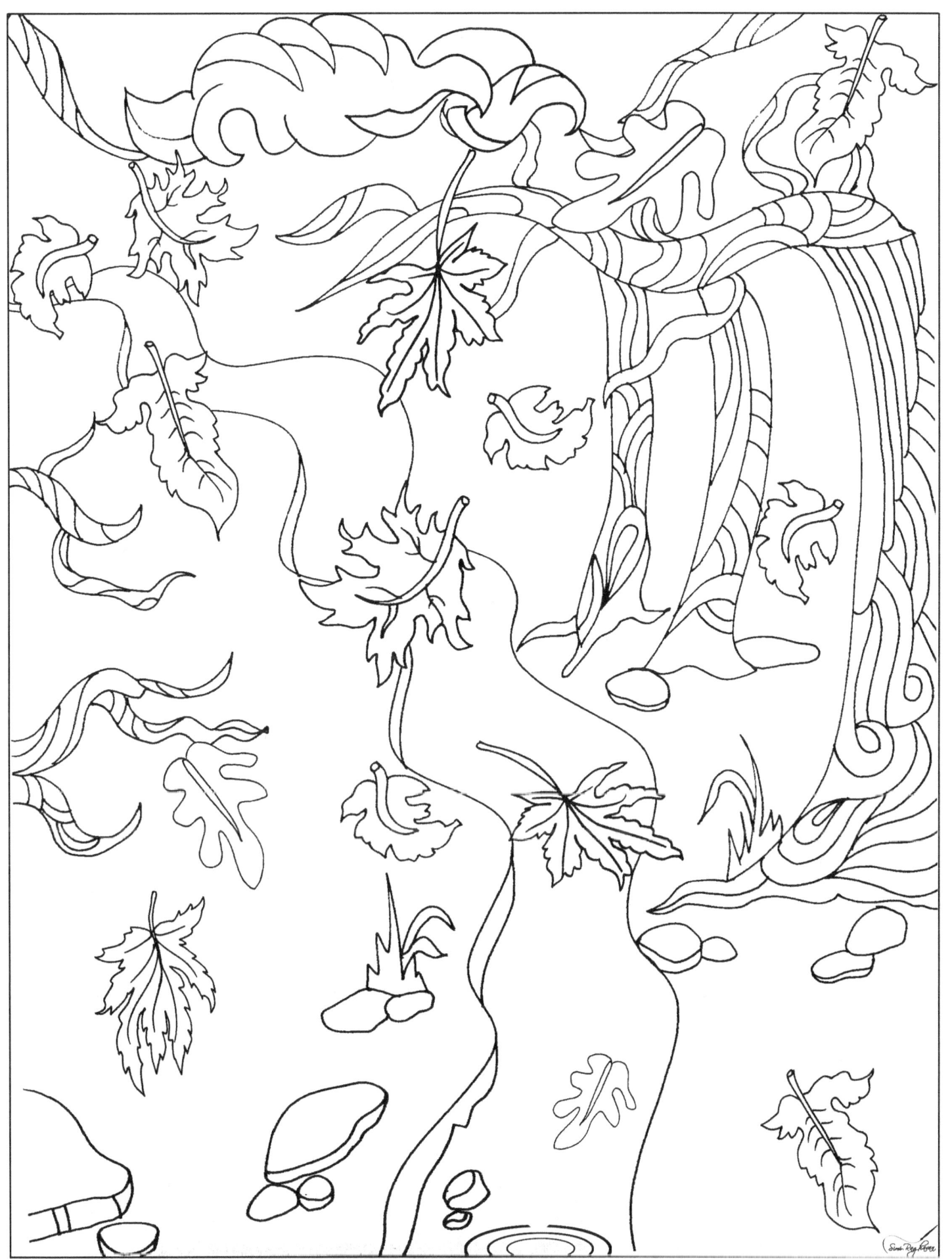

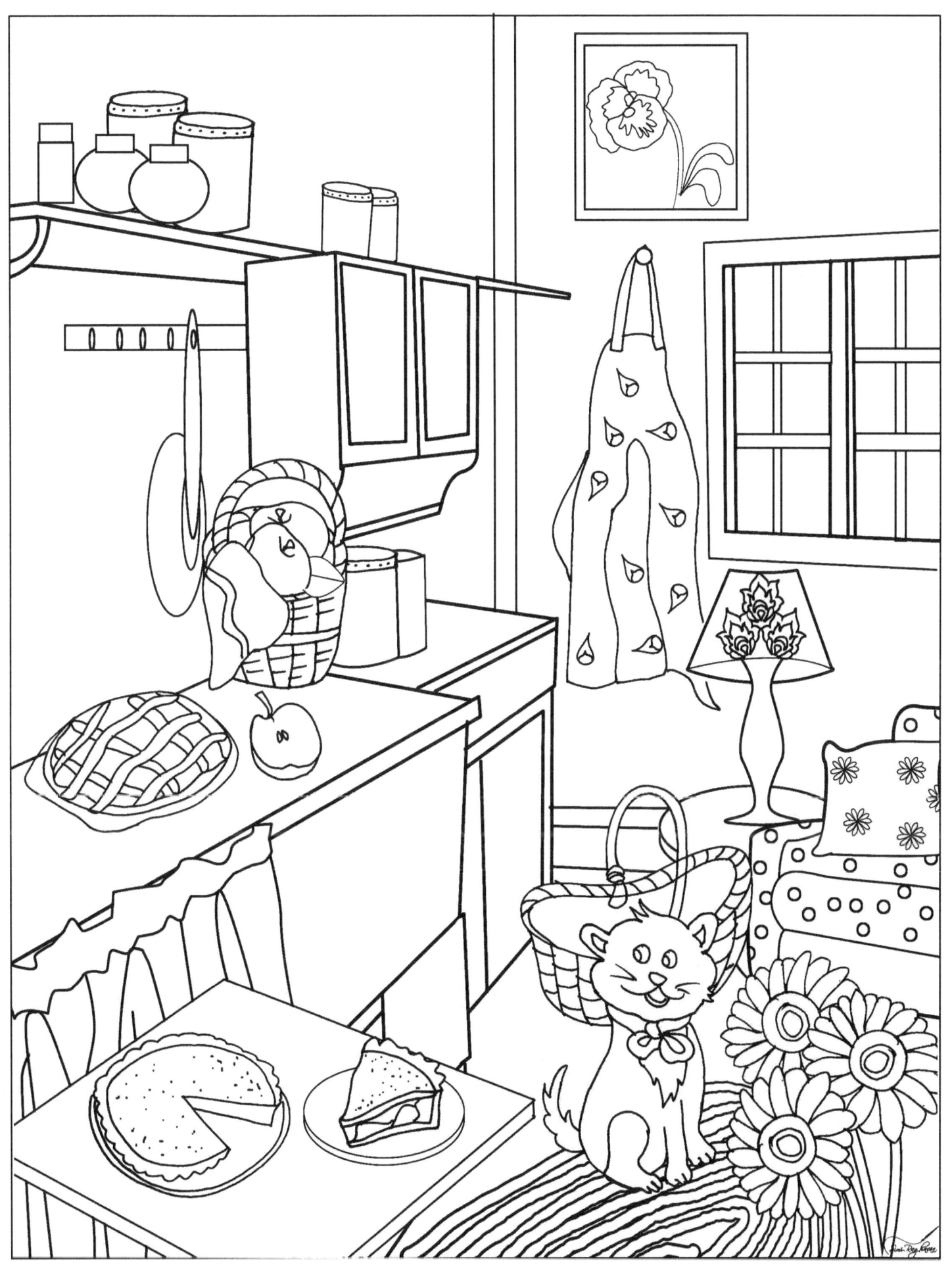

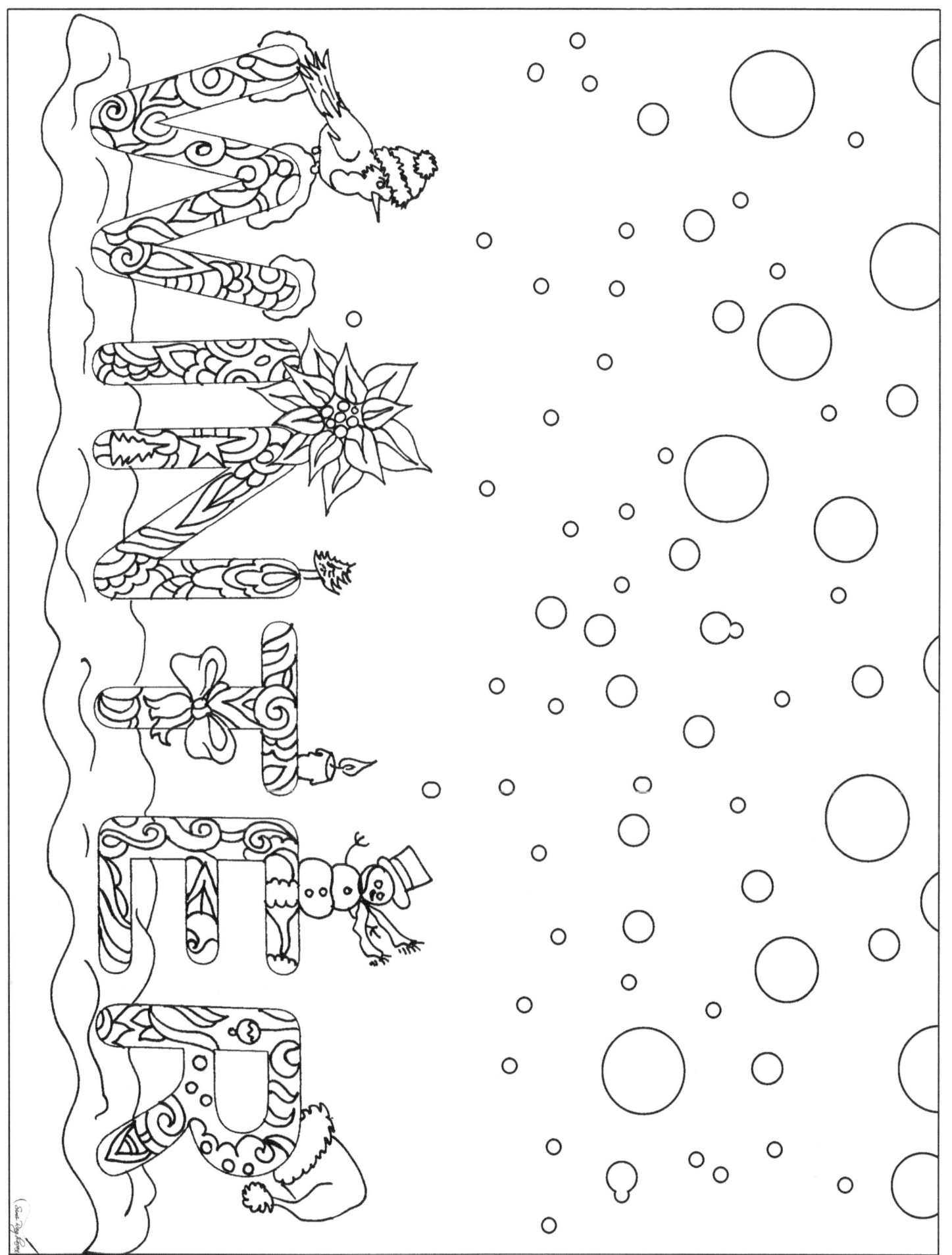

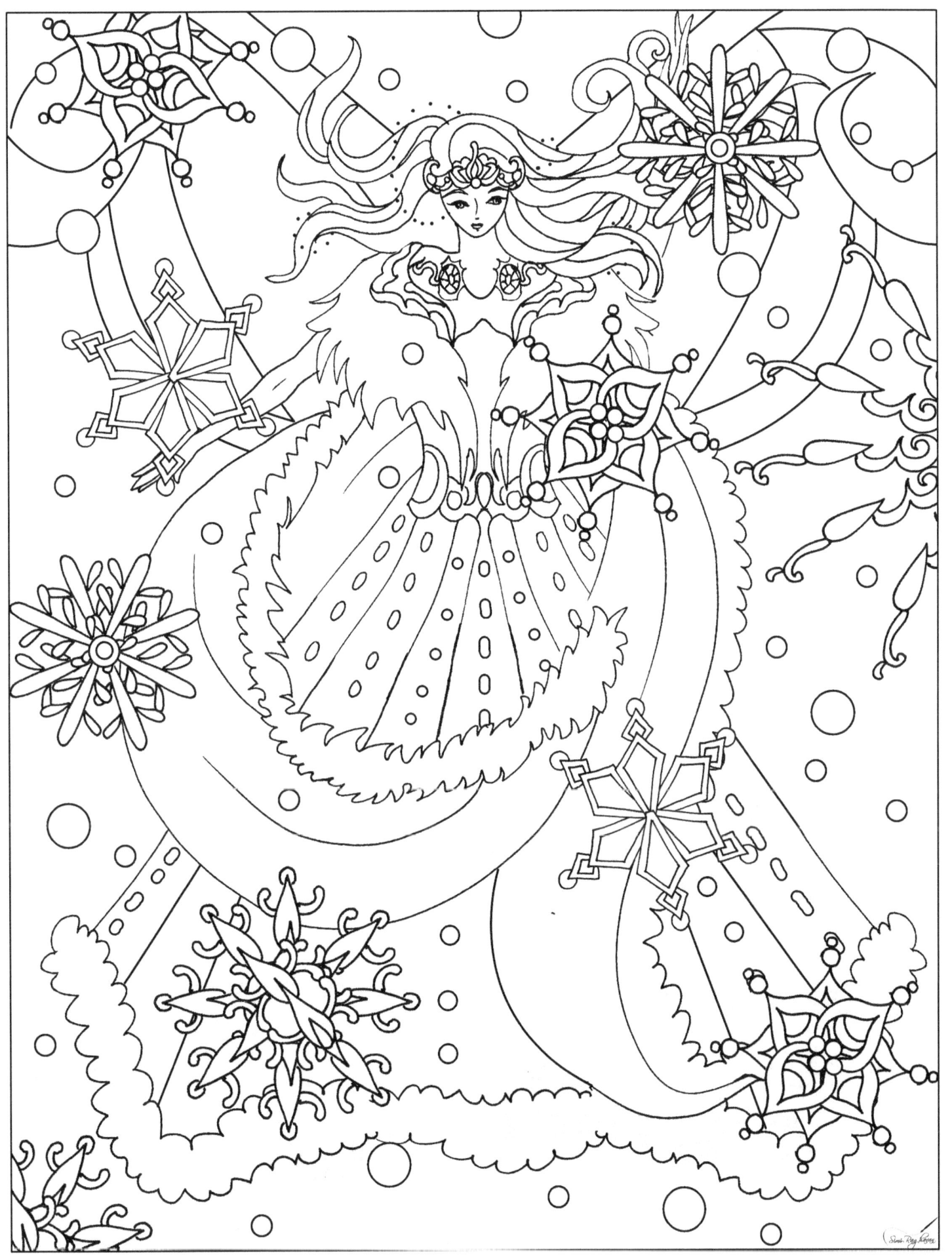

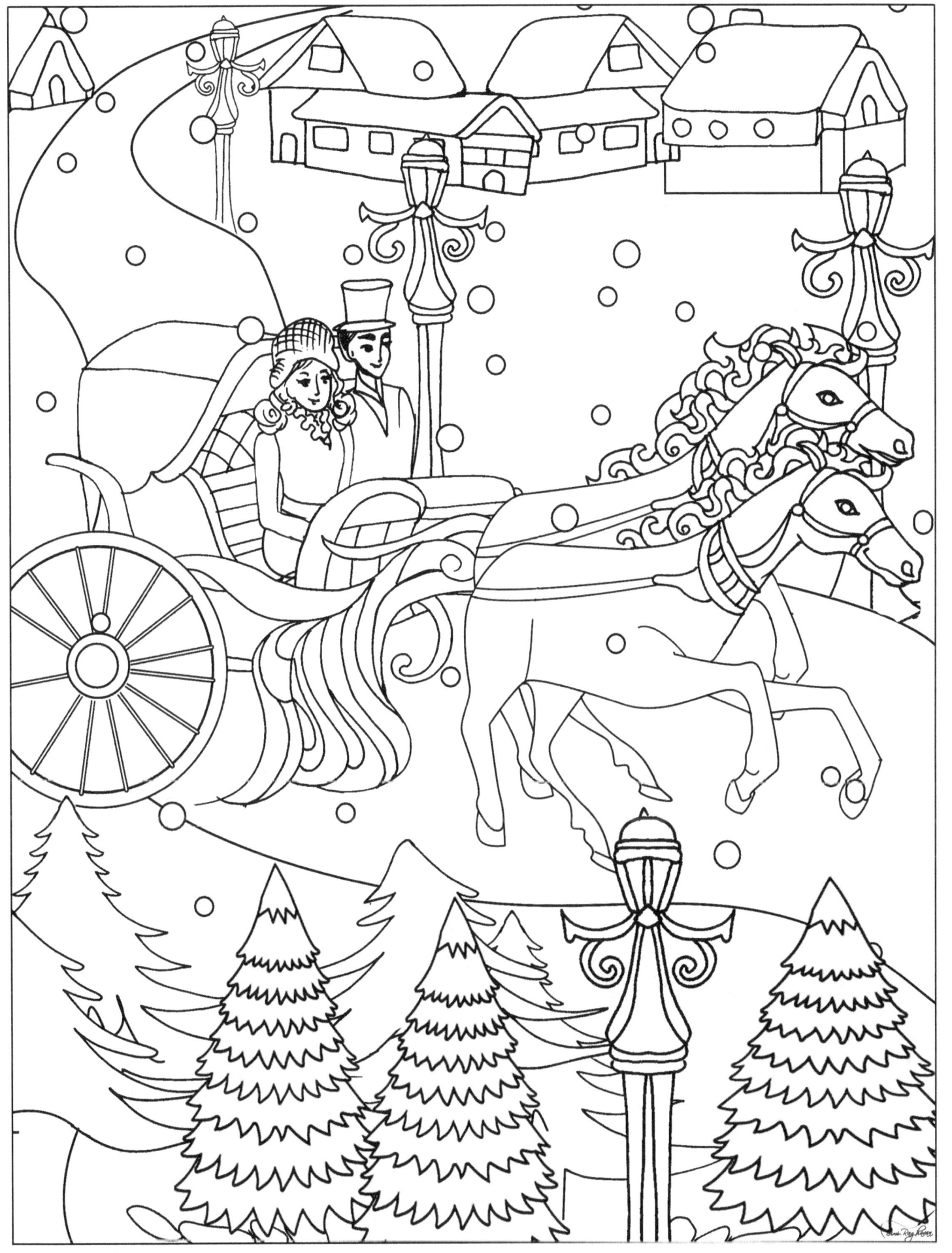

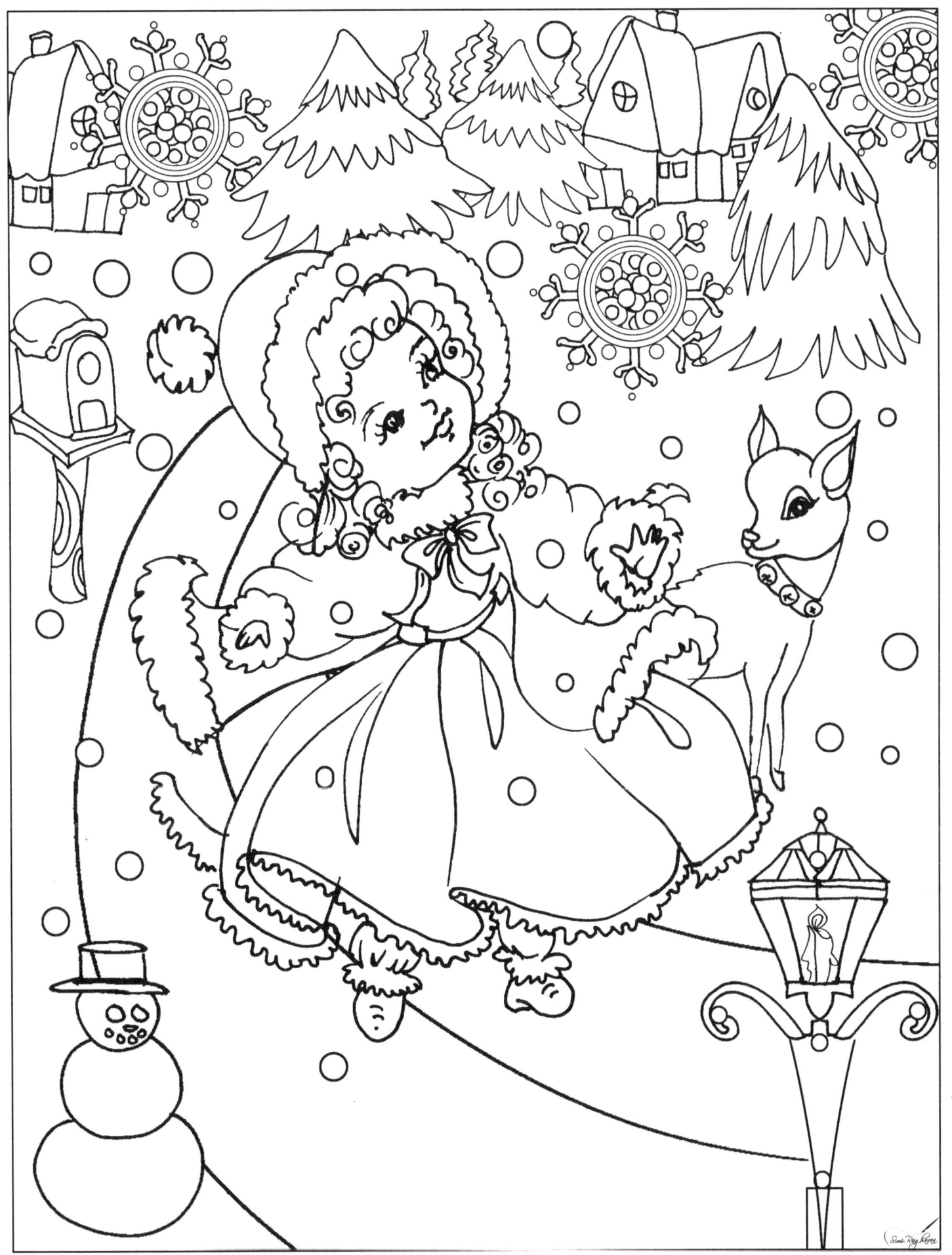

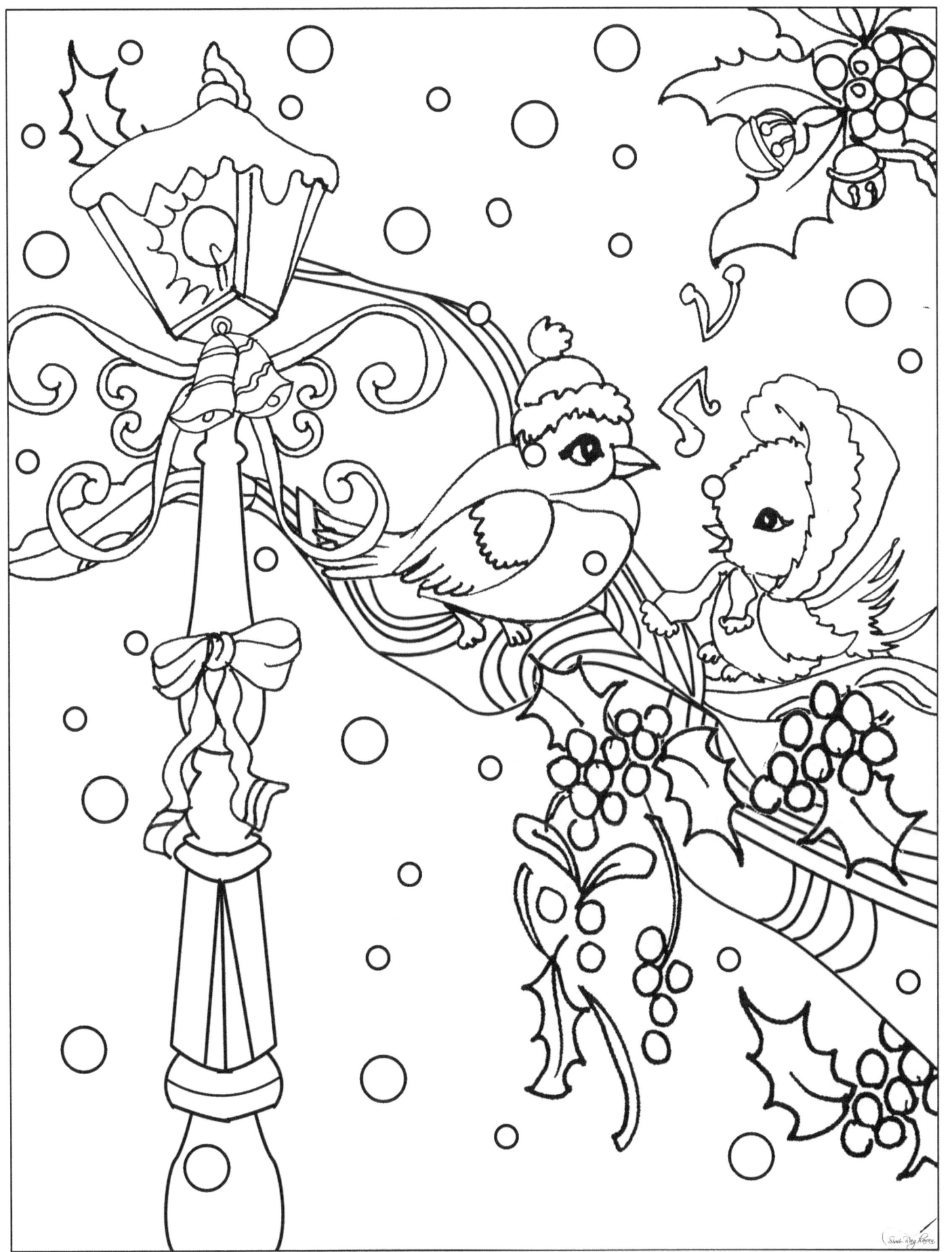

www.ingramcontent.com/pod-product-compliance
Lightning Source LLC
Chambersburg PA
CBHW082218220526
45470CB00010B/3222

9781975616489